Mini Artist
Clay Modeling

Toby Reynolds

WINDMILL
BOOKS ™
New York

Published in 2016 by **Windmill Books**, an Imprint of Rosen Publishing
29 East 21st Street, New York, NY 10010

Models made by Fiona Gowen.

Images on pages 4 and 5 © shutterstock.com

Cataloging-in-Publication Data
Reynolds, Toby.
Clay modeling / by Toby Reynolds.
p. cm. — (Mini artists)
Includes index.
ISBN 978-1-4777-5668-3 (pbk.)
ISBN 978-1-4777-5667-6 (6 pack)
ISBN 978-1-4777-5570-9 (library binding)
1. Modeling — Technique — Juvenile literature.
I. Reynolds, Toby. II. Title.
NB1180.R434 2016
731.4'2—d23

Manufactured in the United States of America

CPSIA Compliance Information: Batch # WS15WM: For Further Information contact Rosen Publishing, New York, New York at 1-800-237-9932

Contents

Getting Started

The projects in this book use lots of art materials that you will already have at home. Any missing materials can be found in art shops and stationery stores.

pen caps

Use pen lids to make small circles of clay. Try this method for eyes or spots on animal models.

modeling tools

There are many types of modeling tools. They are used to cut and mold clay into shape.

sharp pencil

A sharp pencil is a useful tool for scoring clay and for creating holes in your models.

plastic cutlery

Try using some plastic cutlery, or other household objects to model your clay.

wax paper

Clay can be messy to work with so it is wise to work on a sheet of wax paper.

rollers

A small, strong glass bottle or jar with smooth sides can be used to roll out clay.

Handy Hint

abcdefg
hijklmn
opqrstu
vwxyz

Use any leftover clay to create the letters from your name. You can use these to make your own colorful name plaque.

There are three types of readily available clay.
Choose the one that you find easiest to work with.

Oven-drying clay	Air-drying clay	Oil-based clay
Models made from this soft and pliable clay can be baked to make them hard.	Air-drying clay models will slowly dry out when exposed to air.	Oil-based clay does not dry out, so it can be reused again and again.

Adorable Owl

To make this adorable owl you will need a selection of modeling clay, a pen cap, and a sharp pencil.

1 Start your model by rolling brown clay into the shape of the owl's body. Try to make the clay nice and even.

2 Use your finger to press the top of the shape. This will create the shape of the ears. Now add a white belly.

3 Use a pen cap to stamp two yellow clay circles for eyes. Press holes into each of the eyes with a sharp pencil.

4 Use gray or black clay to make a small beak. Create some feet too, and score them with a sharp pencil.

5 Take some of your brown clay and create two wings. Press the wings onto the sides of the owl's body.

6 Now you can make a family of owls. Try using different colors and shapes for their bodies, eyes, beaks, and feet.

8

Pretty Pots

For this flower pot you will need air-drying clay, a scoring tool, a roller, and a terracotta flower pot.

1 Make a circle of yellow modeling clay for the sun. Score rays around the outside and press onto your pot.

2 Now make a cloud from white clay. Roll out the clay and mold it into shape. Press it firmly onto the pot.

3 Make the flower stems by rolling thin strips of green clay and pressing them all around the base of the pot.

4 You can now make all of the flowers. Use a circle of orange clay with a smaller circle of yellow on top.

5 Add grass to your pot by making a long flat strip of green clay and pressing it onto the base of the pot.

6 You can try creating other pictures on flower pots. You could also decorate them with fun patterns.

10

Terrific Train

To make this exciting steam train you will need a selection of different colored modeling clay.

1 Start by making the base of the train. Take a piece of blue clay and shape it into a large, flat rectangle.

2 Make a red cube for the train's cab and a yellow cylinder for the engine. Place these clay pieces on your base.

3 Now you can make the train's wheels. Make four circles from black clay and press them into the base.

4 Use some more blue clay to shape a flat square. Place this on top of the red cube as the roof of the cab.

5 Use a pale blue square to make a window for the cab. Add a green shape for the chimney on the engine.

6 Now you have finished modeling your train, you can make some carriages for the train to pull along.

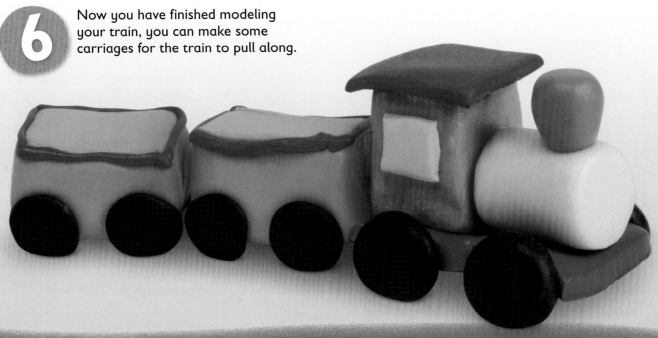

Spotty Dinosaur

To make this dinosaur you will need a selection of colored clay, a pen cap, and a sharp pencil.

1 To start your dinosaur model create a body shape with a pointed end for the tail and another for the neck.

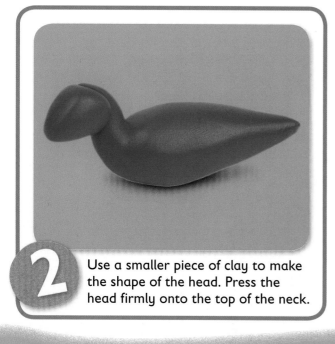

2 Use a smaller piece of clay to make the shape of the head. Press the head firmly onto the top of the neck.

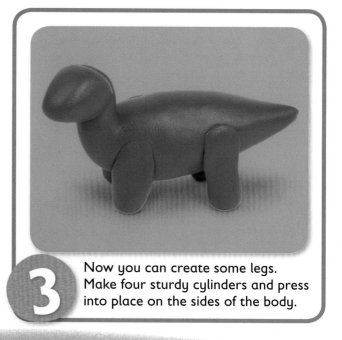

3 Now you can create some legs. Make four sturdy cylinders and press into place on the sides of the body.

4 Use a pen cap to press out two white clay circles for eyes. Make a small hole in each eye with a sharp pencil.

5 Use the pen cap to press out small circles of clay for spots on the body and a row of spines along the back.

6 Try using different combinations of colors and patterns to make a small group of dinosaur models.

Rapid Racer

To make this super-speedy racing car you will need a selection of different colored modeling clay.

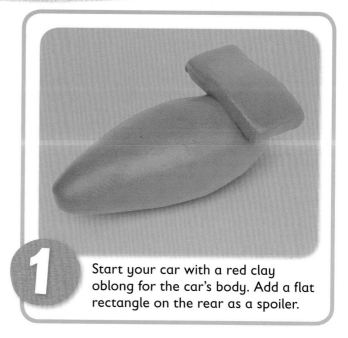

1 Start your car with a red clay oblong for the car's body. Add a flat rectangle on the rear as a spoiler.

2 Now make the four wheels from circles of black clay. Press the wheels firmly onto both sides of the car.

3 Now roll a ball of black clay for the driver's helmet. Add a pale blue visor and place on the racing car.

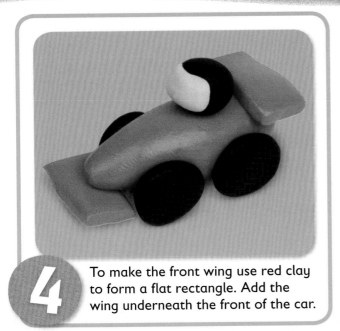

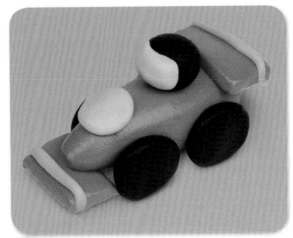

4 To make the front wing use red clay to form a flat rectangle. Add the wing underneath the front of the car.

5 To decorate your racer, add yellow clay stripes to the spoiler and wing, and a big circle on top of the hood.

6 Try using different colors to make more racing cars. You could even add some numbers to their hoods.

Playful Penguin

To make this penguin you will need black, white, and yellow clay, a roller, a pen cap, and a sharp pencil.

1 Start your penguin by making a pear shape from black clay. Add a white section for the penguin's tummy.

2 Use yellow clay to make two small flat shapes for the penguin's feet. Add them to the base of the body.

3 Now make a base for your penguin to stand on. Roll out a circle of white clay and place the penguin on top.

4 Use a pen cap to stamp two white circles for eyes. Press holes in them with a pencil. Add a yellow beak.

5 Now use some of the black clay to make two wings. Attach them to each side of your penguin's body.

6 You can now make a whole family of penguins. Experiment with different body shapes and sizes.

Crazy Monster

To make this monster pencil topper you will need a selection of clay, two pencils, and a pen cap.

1 Start your monster pencil topper by rolling a ball of green clay and pushing it onto the end of a pencil.

2 Use a small piece of green clay for the monster's nose. Then roll two horns and place them on the head.

3 Use a pen cap to stamp out two white circles for eyes. Press holes into each eye with a sharp pencil.

4 Use the sharp pencil again to score a mouth into your monster's face. Add two triangles for the fangs.

5 Now you can add the monster's hair. Roll out some white clay thinly and place strands all around the head.

6 Now you can make a group of friendly monsters. Try using various colors, mouth shapes, and eyes.

Lovely Ladybug

To make these cute little ladybug models you will need a selection of clay, a pen cap, and a sharp pencil.

1 Start your model by making the ladybug's body. Roll a piece of red clay into a large oval shape.

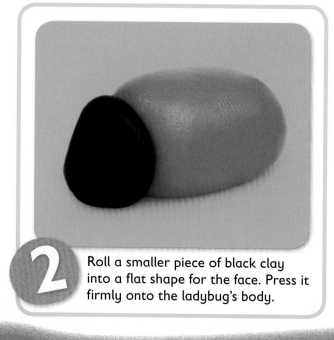

2 Roll a smaller piece of black clay into a flat shape for the face. Press it firmly onto the ladybug's body.

3 Use a pen cap to stamp out two white circles for eyes. Press holes into the eyes with a sharp pencil.

4 Use the sharp pencil again to score a line all the way down the ladybug's back. This shows the two wings.

5 Now you can decorate the wings. Use a pen cap to press out circles of clay and press them into place.

6 Try making some more lovely ladybugs. You can use a variety of colors to make them all different.

Kooky Robot

To make this robot model you will need a selection of clay, a cutting tool, a pen cap, and a sharp pencil.

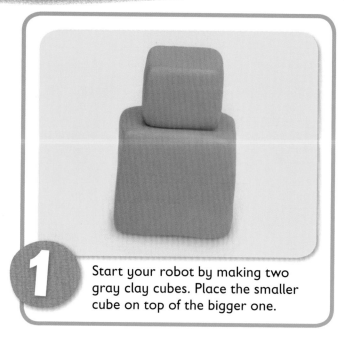

1 Start your robot by making two gray clay cubes. Place the smaller cube on top of the bigger one.

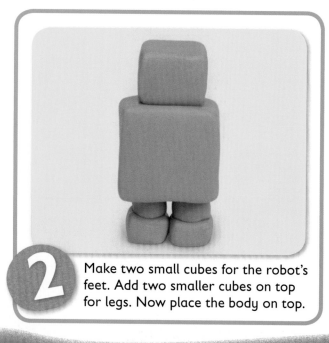

2 Make two small cubes for the robot's feet. Add two smaller cubes on top for legs. Now place the body on top.

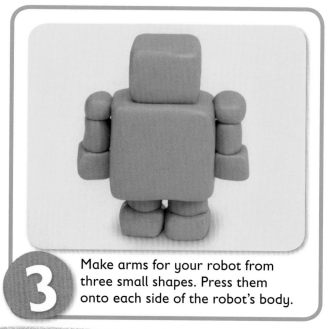

3 Make arms for your robot from three small shapes. Press them onto each side of the robot's body.

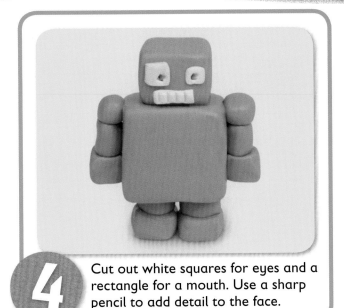

4 Cut out white squares for eyes and a rectangle for a mouth. Use a sharp pencil to add detail to the face.

5 Add a gray square for the control panel. Use a pen cap to stamp out three colorful clay circles for lights.

6 Now you can make more robots using different colors. Experiment with different shapes and sizes.

Glossary

plaque a flat piece of metal used for decoration

pliable supple enough to bend freely or repeatedly without breaking

spines stiff, pointed parts growing from an animal, such as a dinosaur

spoiler a part on a vehicle that uses airflow to create downforce that keeps the car from lifting off the road at high speeds

stationery materials for writing or typing

strand a single thin length of something such as hair, thread, fiber, or wire, especially as twisted together with others

terracotta a glazed or unglazed fired clay often used for pots or roofing

Index

Further Reading

Cook, Trevor, and Sally Henry. *Eco-Crafts.* New York: Rosen Publishing, 2011.

Llimos, Anna. *Earth-Friendly Clay Crafts in 5 Easy Steps.* New York: Enslow, 2014.

Websites

For web resources related to the subject of this book, go to:
www.windmillbooks.com/weblinks and select this book's title.